HELPERS IN OUR COMMUNITY

BAKERS

CHRISTINE HONDERS

PowerKiDS press

New York

Published in 2020 by The Rosen Publishing Group, Inc.
29 East 21st Street, New York, NY 10010

First Edition

Editor: Greg Roza
Book Design: Reann Nye

Photo Credits: Cover, p.1 Diana Haronis Marc Romanelli/Getty Images; pp. 4–22 Abstractor/Shutterstock.com; p. 5 LightFieldStudios/iStoc /Getty Images Plus/Getty Images; p. 7 Chamille White/Shutterstock.com; p. 9 Jerry U/Shutterstock.com; p. 11 LightField Studios/Shutterstock.com; p. 13 antoniodiaz/Shutterstock.com; p. 15 Monty Rakusen/Cultura/Getty Images; p. 17 Dusan Petkovic/Shutterstock.com; p. 19 Hero Images/Getty Images; p. 21 Iliana Mestari/ Moment/Getty Images; p. 22 LightField Studios/Shutterstock.com.

Library of Congress Cataloging-in-Publication Data

Names: Honders, Christine, author.
Title: Bakers / Christine Honders.
Description: New York : PowerKids Press, [2020] | Helpers in our community | Includes index.
Identifiers: LCCN 2019011625| ISBN 9781725308022 (pbk.) | ISBN 9781725308046 (library bound) | ISBN 9781725308039 (6 pack)
Subjects: LCSH: Baking. | Cookies. | Pies. | Pastry. | Bread.
Classification: LCC TX763 .H5866 2020 | DDC 641.81/5-dc23
LC record available at https://lccn.loc.gov/2019011625

Manufactured in the United States of America

CPSIA Compliance Information: Batch #CWPK20. For Further Information contact Rosen Publishing, New York, New York at 1-800-237-9932.

CONTENTS

The Neighborhood Bakery

Many neighborhoods have a bakery. The smells hit you when you walk in the door. There are many choices: rolls, bread, pies, and cookies. There may be beautiful birthday cakes to buy. Who's the person who makes all these yummy goodies? It's the baker!

The Basics of Baking

People make baked goods by mixing **ingredients** and heating them in an oven. Bakers make bread by mixing **flour**, water, salt, and **yeast**. Have you ever noticed that bread is full of small holes? A gas created by yeast makes those holes.

Baking History

The **ancient** Egyptians first made baking an art form. In ancient Rome, bakers had very high social positions! By the early 1900s, people went to their neighborhood bakery to buy what they needed for the day. Today, most people buy bread made in factories.

bread oven
ancient Rome

What Bakers Do

Bakers know lots of **recipes**. They measure and mix the ingredients to make **dough** for their treats. They roll and **knead** the dough. They set the oven to the right **temperature**. They don't want their bread or other treats to burn!

Your Neighborhood Baker

Neighborhood bakers work in small bakeries. Some work in grocery stores. They make many different baked goods for people to buy. Bakers also make treats for parties. If you want a cake that says "Happy Birthday, Grandma!" on it, call the baker!

Commercial Bakers

Commercial bakers work in factories. They bake things in large amounts. These items are sent to stores around the world. Commercial bakers make lots of baked goods quickly. They know how to use large mixing machines and ovens. They make sure the ingredients they use are safe to eat.

LIFT THIS FLAP
16kg net

Becoming a Baker

Bakers use math to measure ingredients. They learn how to take care of food so that it doesn't make people sick. Some bakers go to cooking school. Some learn on the job with a baker who's been doing the job a long time.

More Than Making Cookies

Baking is science! If you don't follow a recipe right, it might not work. If you use the wrong ingredients or temperature, your cookies could look (and taste) like hockey pucks! Bakers are scientists who test recipes to make sure they're perfect.

The Art of Baking

Some bakers want their cakes to look as good as they taste. They make cakes that don't even look like cakes! They use special tools to turn sugar and chocolate into flowers, trees, or animals. These bakers turn their cakes into works of art!

Baking a Better Community

Bakers often work from early in the morning until late at night. But seeing the smile on a person's face when they come to pick up their goodies makes it worthwhile. Bakers are an important part of our community. They bake things that make people happy!

GLOSSARY

ancient: From a time long ago.

commercial: Having to do with the buying or selling of goods or services.

dough: A mixture of flour and other ingredients used to make bread, cookies, or other things.

flour: A powder made from a grain and used in cooking.

ingredient: One of the things that make up a mixture.

knead: To press with your hands.

recipe: A set of instructions for making a food dish.

temperature: How hot or cold something is.

yeast: Single-celled living things that are needed to make bread and other foods.

INDEX

WEBSITES

Due to the changing nature of Internet links, PowerKids Press has developed an online list of websites related to the subject of this book. This site is updated regularly. Please use this link to access the list: www.powerkidslinks.com/HIOC/bakers